Real Estate Agent

CEMETERY

How to Survive the Fears, Challenges, and Mistakes That Can Kill Your Real Estate Career

---

Christie Ellis

Real Estate Agent Cemetery

Cover designed by Guerrero Media Group

Christie Ellis
Realtor ®, Designated Broker,
Coach & Speaker
Christie@ChristieEllis.com

Dedication

This book is dedicated to my amazing family who helped me become the person I am today. I greatly appreciate your never-ending love and support.

Praise for Real Estate CEMETERY

"There's a vast number of potentially *hugely successful, profitable and value-based real estate agents who never got there because they quit before ever breaking through from fear to knowledge. What a shame that is! However, thanks to Christie Ellis and her new small book with HUGE wisdom, this need not happen to you. Christie will take you by the hand and guide you through your opening first few weeks so that you can obtain the knowledge you need to go from confused newbie to confident and powerful agent. The result? More fun, less stress, more profit, and referrals coming at you faster than you can handle them (but, you'll find a way)."*

- Bob Burg, coauthor of, *The Go-Giver* and
Endless Referrals
www.burg.com

An amazing resource for new Real Estate Agents! Using real-world stories and examples, Christie will help you navigate the challenges, leverage the opportunities, develop a vision and grow in confidence. From the first page, you'll recognize the authentic voice of a Real Estate Mentor who has gone before you to mark the path with systems, resources, wisdom and encouragement. This book is generous in spirit and filled with experience. Bravo Christie!

--Dondi Scumaci, Author of *Designed for Success, Ready, Set...Grow and Career Moves*
www.DondiScumaci.com

I have read many books over the years about being a successful Real Estate agent and the timing could not have been better for Christie's new book titled "Real Estate Agent Cemetery" to hit the streets. Most books offer closing techniques and gimmicks to build a business and that's where Christie separates herself from the pack. She states that there are no secrets to being a successful Real Estate agent and then gives you proven steps in achieving your goals. The steps she offers are simple, but don't let the simplicity fool you. What is easy to do is also easy not to do. What I appreciate the most is that not only does she talk the talk, but she walks the walk and as a fellow Real Estate business owner, THAT IS HUGE. I will highly recommend this book to every one of my agents.

-Mike Benton *Home Towne Real Estate, Owner* and *Change Coach*
www.mikebentonenterprises.com

Introduction

When I first became a real estate agent I was scared to death of getting a contract. I said to myself, "I don't know enough, I am going to mess this up and get sued." What a way to start a career! When it came time to writing my first contract I asked for help and paid close attention to be sure I really understood what I was learning. I crossed all my "t's" and dotted all my "i's." It was beautiful as far as contracts go. I felt empowered.

Then my second contract came. Logically, I thought I could execute the second contract in the same manner as the first one. Makes sense-right? I was so confident, I didn't even ask for help from a mentor, a more experienced agent or my broker.

Big mistake.

My inexperience and overconfidence cost my client $3,000! When it came time to finally sell that house, I felt so guilty for my mistake, I took the listing for free to make up for my mistakes.

That cost me $9,000. Yuk.

Understand that I know the fears and the challenges agents face. I have been there, made the mistakes and lived through it. Even during the last real estate bubble, I have turned tragedy into triumph. I am not alone, of course. Many other agents at many different levels of their careers have also survived and even thrived. Many more have not. In the beginning, there is always an element of fear and reluctance to building a client base and developing a business. Trust me; I was no different than you. The idea of learning all of the legal issues, contracts AND getting out there and competing in one of the most highly competitive markets in the country almost derailed me from starting.

It is always easier, cheaper and less painful to learn from other people's mistakes than learning from your own. I've done both.

Throughout this book are examples of mistakes agents have made and all of them are still in the real estate business! I selected these "zingers" to show you that if we can do it, you most certainly can as well. None of the information, blueprints or ideas are super secret or particularly earth shattering information for that matter. However, by focusing and applying yourself in the basics, you can refocus, face your fears and know we have all been there and survived and so will you.

What I am offering you in this book is a clear and easy to understand philosophy and the system for getting started. This book is only the beginning. This book will help you start off in the right direction. Many of you will simply skim it, read it, nod your head and go about your day.

The winners will apply it.

In the spirit of keeping things simple, memorize the following acroynm, KCGCR. Whenever you get stuck, lose a deal or are complaining that the market is dead, like Michael Jordan and thousands of athletes will profess, go back to the basics. There are 5 important life saving techniques I call the **Critical Care Success System:**

1. Knowledge
2. Confidence
3. Goal Setting
4. Communication
5. Relationships

When you focus on these basics, in good times or in bad, you will always be doing what is right. All businesses work best when the owners take a long-term view. By focusing on these basics, you will most certainly be in the top 1% of agents worldwide. (Ask any top producer and they will nod their head in agreement)

NOTE: If you are reading these career saving techniques and think, "I'd rather you just pull the plug." Don't do it. You can learn these skills.

Let me fill you in on a little secret. Nothing separates the exceptional agent from the mediocre agent in terms of "born talent" or personality. Every single skill we discuss is a learned skill which you can become proficient at in record time.

I had to learn some of them myself. I am going to cast pride to the wind and share not only my successes, but my goof ups, too. By sharing many of my experiences with you, I would like to help you avoid those mistakes and become positive and profitable faster than I did. There are no trade secrets. They simply don't exist. Secrets are a myth. There are more than enough clients to go around. The ones you find and serve properly will stay with you, so long as you continuously provide value.

At the end of some sections I will recommend further reading and specific professional people to connect with that will help you continue a healthy way of practicing real estate. By no means are they the only people to connect with (some will actually be applicable to more than one section). However, the list provided is a great place to start. Additionally, when possible, I am including their Facebook pages for ease of contact.

NOTE: Facebook is a very useful tool and we discuss it a little further along. When you go to their pages, when possible, I gave you a link to their personal page. In some instances, a person's personal page has reached its limit and you must go to their professional page.

(Hint: Do you have a professional page, yet?)

OMG – Did It Kill Her Career?

I had a buyer and I needed to request an extension of the inspection period. The listing agent said, "sure thing, I will send the paperwork tonight." I didn't receive the paperwork and asked for it again. Now, it is the day the inspection period ends. He assured me again, "no problem, I will get it to you. We had some technical difficulties." I understand that, I can wait.

The day after the period ends I am talking to the agent, he mentioned something about issues with the house. I mentioned that we have a few extra days because he agreed to it. His comment was, "you never did get that paperwork did you?" I said no, "but you said..." Then he replied, "yes but I never sent it to you in writing." Ouch! That hurt.

I should have cancelled or sent some request for repairs, but I didn't. That one cost me my client's earnest money. My fault so I had to pay him back. Now – I NEVER, no matter how much I trust the other agent, do anything without it in writing.

Critical Care Success System
Career Saving Technique of:

Gaining Knowledge

When I first started my real estate career, and for sometime afterwards, I thought what I was taught is school WAS EVERYTHING I needed to know. Perhaps you are ahead of me in this area and you know that learning is a lifelong process. When I began my real estate career, I felt so overwhelmed with all the new information I didn't know where to start. When I reflect on the past, I realize that I hadn't read enough books on real estate or business in general. I hadn't attended any seminars. I came to find out that school teaches you the basics and life gives you the rest. I needed to learn that real estate was *my* business and not my broker's. It took me a minute before I realized I was truly working for myself!

There are three important concepts you need to be proficient and knowledgeable about when it comes to real estate:

1. The industry and the current trends
2. How to build a real estate business
3. Your clients true needs and wants

Industry Knowledge

There are so many fantastic resources for tracking sales trends, market trends, legislation, etc. that it can make your head spin. Add to that the specifics on what will affect home buying or selling, lending rules, and learning what is going on in your local market and nationally and you should qualify for a PHD in real estate! It is tremendously important to learn what is going on in your local market so you can answer questions intelligently, and with valid information. When a prospect or customer asks you a market specific question, the worst thing you can do is make up answers when you don't have one. It is ALWAYS much better to say you aren't sure and you will research that information and get back to them.

Follow through.

I recommend getting together a group of people, about 6 to 8, that are active in the real estate market who are not only real estate agents. Seek out other professionals as well such as, lenders, title reps, appraisers, and start a mastermind group. A mastermind is a terrific and inexpensive method to keep up on current trends, share ideas and even garner some leads. People always do business with other people they know, like and trust. By getting together on a consistent basis with your peers, you will form a team that has terrific bonding power. Sure, you may "know" a title officer or have a few favorite mortgage brokers. But, with a mastermind, you will get to know these professionals more intimately. You will keep up to date on various aspects of the industry, have people hold you accountable to your wants and needs, and be able to learn from each other.

I have participated in my mastermind for years. I can assure you the time invested has been returned 10 fold. Writing this book is one example.

In addition to masterminds, attend seminars hosted by your local board, title agency, attorney or any other individual or organization you may find. It will enable you to stay on top of any changes your state is making to contracts, new federal and state laws that will affect how you run your business, changes to short sale policies, disclosure laws, ethics laws and codes of conduct.

I have elevated my mastermind to a level where, quite often, I am called to consult, mentor and even speak on some of these topics. For details, visit www.ChristieEllis.com.

Here are some resources for you to look into to help with your gaining industry knowledge.

Websites
www.RealEstateAgentSuccessCircle.com
www.realtor.org
www.inman.com
www.money.cnn.com/real_estate
www.agbeat.com

Blogs
www.activerain.com
www.therealestatebloggers.com
www.amyswaneycmb.blogspot.com

People/Organizations to follow on Social Media
www.facebook.com/realtors
https://www.facebook.com/groups/RaiseTheBar

Also, look for your local real estate board's social media page. Ask your mastermind who else they use for staying on top of their game.

Knowledge of How to Build a Business

There is more to building a business than what I am going to tell you here, but I didn't want to make your head explode. I want to give you some basic ideas that you may have forgotten or perhaps not yet realized. From this foundation, you can start the building process to a lucrative and exciting career. I highly recommend you hire a business coach to take it to the next level and continue building your business.

NOTE: I don't recommend anything that I don't do myself. In addition to belonging to a terrific mastermind, I have a business coach. You need to get one as well.

I don't know too many realtors who have taken the all important step of writing a business plan. A business plan? Are you serious?

Yes.

For starters, the moment you commit to being a business owner (which you are) you are making a statement embracing your entrepreneurism. Without a blueprint (business plan) and without a destination (goals) how will you know if you are where you could be. How will you know what to modify, change or celebrate?

Start writing a business plan and answer the following questions:

- How much do you need to spend monthly to run your business?
- Who is your competition?
- Do you have a niche market?
- What is your growth plan?
- How will you advertise your services?

All these are questions you need to answer so you understand where you need to focus your time and energy. Did you write them down? No? You must be one of the 95% who simply read and nod their head...OK. Good luck with that.

If you are part of the 5% who take their business seriously, take a few minutes and WRITE DOWN YOUR ANSWERS. (Bold for emphasis only. I'm not yelling at you...well, maybe a little)

Seek out a SCORE counselor in your area at www.SCORE.org. They are a group of 13,000 mentor volunteers who have succeeded in their field and now donate their time to assist entrepreneurs, at no cost to you. They can help you with your business plan and your marketing plan. What a valuable resource.

Second, find a broker that fits your specific needs. This is a very important step in building your business. From large scale firms to small independents, they both have their pros and cons. Interview brokers in different size companies, ask them:

- What they do to help you grow your business?
- Do they cover your error and omission insurance?
- What is amount will they keep from every commission check?
- What is the deductible for the Errors and Omission insurance if a court case is initiated?
- When are they available if you have questions?
- What rules do you have when it comes to creating your own brand?
- What training do they offer?

These are very important questions to find the answers to when you are looking for a broker to hang your license. Simply signing up with a friend or the closest firm to your house isn't what professional business people do. They seek out and associate with the best. Period.

Ideally you will want a broker who can assist you with as much as you need. This is especially true if you are a new agent; you may need training or individual mentorship. Look for a broker who will be available in urgent situations and when you need an answer sooner rather than later. Be sure the fees the broker charges will allow you to afford your monthly bills, and one who has an E&O (errors and omissions) insurance deductible that is within your budget.

Don't simply interview the broker to see if they meet your needs, however. It is important to show all of the brokers you interview that you are not just another warm body to sit at a desk and fail like 95% of the other agents they've hired. Pull out your business plan and show them you are part of the 5%. Show them that you are taking this business very seriously and you plan on being a top performer. (See? That business plan isn't simply to keep you on track; it can be used to let your broker know you are there to work)

Third, you should create a brand and a logo that represents you. You should find out if your broker requires certain colors in your logo. Be sure that you create something that sets you apart from the others. It can be as simple as your name in a particular font and color to having a graphic artist design something. Whatever it is, spend some time (and a little bit of money if you aren't creative) in making the brand effective. This is something people will see and if it looks cheap they will think *you* are cheap. Always be sure you have your broker's approval on all final concepts. You can get designer very inexpensively from:

www.elance.com
www.odesk.com
www.guru.com
www.99designs.com

A logo is just the start of creating who you are and positioning yourself as the expert. You need to start thinking of your brand. As my friend Bill Ellis (no relation ☺) of Branding for Results says, "a logo is not a brand. A catchy saying is not a brand. Your brand is your value proposition, your promise to the public, your reputation…in short your brand is the intangible sum of your attributes. Know your purpose, seek perspective, exercise patience and watch your brand thrive."

Create a benefit statement. This is a 5 to 7 second statement that answers the question, "so what do you do?" If you say, "I am a real estate agent" nobody will care. It's boring. When you create a benefit statement, design a clear and emotional benefit to whoever is listening to you. You get bonus points if it causes a question. Mine is: "I guide people comfortably through the process of buying or selling a home." It is short, easy and a lot nicer. By adding the adjectives "comfortably"

I've created an emotional cushion in an otherwise stressful situation (moving).

Protect yourself from liability and taxes. Establish a professional entity that will keep your personal assets separate from your business assets. You are in business for yourself. Treat it with respect. It is exceedingly simple to set up an LLC, corporation to separate you personal life from your business life. It is a very inexpensive way to protect your assets. Contact your CPA or an attorney to see what he/she recommends for your particular situation. A quick Google search will uncover thousands of choices, as well.

One of the last items and one of the most important, is your presence on social media and the Internet. Hopefully, you already have a web page (either individually or with your broker). You definitely will need a social media presence in order to successfully position yourself online. At a bare minimum be on Facebook, Twitter, LinkedIn and have a personal website. Bonus points if you blog, set up an ActiveRain profile (www.activerain.com), have a hub page and contribute to your chamber of commerce's newsletter.

There are thousands of social media experts who have some great advice. I want to make one idea crystal clear.

You are not on social media to promote yourself.

Social media is SOCIAL! Think of social media as a back yard barbeque. People gather round and chat, share funny stories and ask about the kids. It's called social media for a reason. Sure, their business pages and blogs are important, but when people spend 90% of the time talking about themselves, don't you get bored? Don't you avoid reading those pages?

What makes you think your site is any different?

People are looking here to get to know you. You want to add value to people's lives, post things people will find helpful. You can start with stories and ideas that are helpful and/or interesting. For example, post an article on decluttering your house or how to spruce up a room with things you already own. You want people to know you as a resource and that you keep your "fans" engaged. Ask THEM for ideas. Get people to respond to your posts. The more replies, comments and interaction you receive, the better.

Social media is not a replacement for getting out and meeting people. Nothing will build your business faster and stronger than the personal relationships you create and build. In fact, the next time you look at your emails, separate the ones you read vs. the ones you discard without reading. Chances are, most of the ones you actually read are from people you have met face to face. At the very least, you've had a conversation with them.

15

A website is also important, and they don't have to be expensive. Here is where you can be more "sales-y". Keep giving away fresh content and helpful advice, but once you've engaged a person and they've visited your professional website, they are probably looking for a real estate agent now or in the near future. Let them see what is available in the market. Show your listings. Publish some testimonials and plenty of pictures. Bonus if you can post a few videos of satisfied customers when they are happily in the new home you sold them.

Be sure to publish a blog. You don't have to be a writer or a web geek to put up a blog. In fact, it is free or nearly free to publish one. Here are a few ideas:

- Write about the questions you hear most often, i.e. what is a short sale? What is the difference between buying a short sale or a bank owned home?
- Take a photo of something in your farm area and write about it as it pertains to the neighborhood.
- Write about market conditions, local events going on
- Review a book. Be honest and read it first!
- Tell a great story of a time when you received awesome customer service.

They can be as long or short as you like, but too long and you will lose most people.

Video has been dominating the internet recently and most likely for a long time. If you don't enjoy writing, publish a weekly video blog. A video blog is the same as a regular blog only it is you speaking about a topic. If you aren't comfortable on camera, put together a slide show of homes or a PowerPoint presentation, record it and post it. They add to the experience of learning about who you are and what you are like.

A few things to NEVER do on social media:

- Insult or rant about anything or anyone
- Post details no one needs to know about
- Share *too* much personal information

Use common sense when posting on social media outlets. Remember your clients can find you on social media as easily as anyone. What image are you portraying? Want to see mine? For details, visit www.ChristieEllis.com

Books
Endless Referrals by Bob Burg
Career Moves by Dondi Scumaci
Book Yourself Solid by Michael Port
The Millionaire Real Estate Agent by Gary Keller
Less Blah Blah More Aha, Ken Brand

Websites
www.myownbusiness.org

www.entrepreneur.com
www.score.org
www.technospheric.com
www.wordpress.org

Blogs
www.burg.com/blog
www.mikebentonenterprises.com/mike-benton-enterprises-blog
www.brandingforresults.com/category/blog

People/Organizations to follow on Social Media
www.facebook.com/burgbob
www.facebook.com/tpillars
www.facebook.com/mikewbenton
www.facebook.com/pages/Dondi-Scumaci/45412576283
www.facebook.com/BarefootExecutive
www.facebook.com/bill.ellis
www.facebook.com/yourlinkedinexpert
www.facebook.com/courtneyengle

Knowledge of Your Client's Wants and Needs

This, of course, will be specific to each and every client. The reason for mentioning this is because we all need to be aware of what we do for, and say to, our clients. One major pitfall we often get trapped in is that we take our past experiences with clients and apply that experience to every other client.

Each experience is unique to every new person you meet, so never assume anything.

18

Always ask questions, clarify anything you may be unsure of, listen to what your clients are discussing in regards to location, types of homes, what is a must for them. The agent that spends the most time getting to know their client's wants and needs will never lack for referrals. Don't be afraid to offer suggestions but don't be pushy or think you know better than they do, most especially do not ever assume that you know what they want. Always make it about them.

OMG – Did it Kill Her Career?

Every once in a while we say things or assume things without thinking of how our words may affect someone. Margery Berbling, of Hometown USA Realty in Chandler, AZ, had that happen to her. A new client came into her office and he mentioned he worked at a local college. She assumed things based on his appearance and asked, "are you in the maintenance department?" With that he replied, "no, I am a professor." Margie quickly realized she inadvertently and unintentionally judged him by an outward appearance and apologized profusely. Fortunately for her he was a kind man who was not offended and to this day they are good friends.

Margie's lesson learned was that no matter what someone is wearing, what kind of car they drive; don't assume to know the answers. Always allow people to tell their story before you begin helping them. If you prejudge someone, you could be wrong, and cause a very awkward situation for both you and the client.

Books
The Go-Giver by Bob Burg and John David Mann
The Art of Persuasion by Bob Burg
Getting Naked by Patrick Lencioni
Up, Down or Sideways by Mark Sanborn

Blogs
www.burg.com/blog
www.marksanborn.com/blog

People/Organizations to follow on Social Media
www.facebook.com/DixieDynamite
www.facebook.com/burgbob
www.facebook.com/marksanbornspeaks

Critical Care Success System Career Saving Technique of:

Building Confidence

Like gaining knowledge, building confidence in yourself is an ongoing process and the more you continue to learn the more confident you will grow. There is a clear difference between confidence and arrogance. Confidence is positive. It means you know you are capable of handling questions and situations effectively and are able to manage an error if you make one. On the other hand, arrogance is when you answer without knowledge of the topic, when you care less about what your client's wants and more about what suits your needs.

> *"Arrogant people talk about themselves. Confident people allow other people talk about them."*
> -Doug Crowe

Confidence comes from learning how to handle the parts of yourself that scare you the most. Unshakable confidence creates the feeling of comfort with the amount of knowledge you have accumulated. Confidence with wisdom means you know you don't know everything and are confident enough to admit it. There will always be questions you don't have the answers to, but when you have confidence in your knowledge base, you will know to whom and when to find those answers.

Earlier, I confessed about my early mistakes and the self-fulfilling prophecy I created because I kept *telling* myself I was going to mess up. It should not have surprised me that eventually that is precisely what I did.

When I was a new agent, like many of you, I lacked plenty of resources. I didn't know where to gain the information or who to turn to. I didn't feel my broker had enough time for me. I didn't seek out help. I didn't know how to build my sphere of influence. I lacked a mentor. I didn't try to learn from people who were already in the business or who had business knowledge. I was green.

Resources, especially intellectual resources, are so important for starting your career in real estate, it bears repeating.

When in doubt, seek it out.

I want to help you achieve a high level of confidence and not be as freaked out as I was when I first started. Your confidence has to come from within. The confidence you need is not something I can give you. You can't buy it and you can't instantly download confidence into your personality.

Time + experience + patience = confidence

There is no other path other than this formula to get there. You can't "fake it 'till you make it" and you can't wish for it. Confidence comes to those who are humble, coachable and thirsty.

If you are new to your industry, never fear. Your transparency of being new can be used to your advantage. How many times have you sat down at a restaurant and been waited on by two servers? One was in training. Didn't you show that server extra attention? Didn't you reflect on *your* first week on the job?

If you are a new agent, let your clients know that you are new. But don't stop there. Also let them know that as one of your first customers, you are highly motivated to dramatically exceed their expectations. You will be working from referrals and your first few clients will be treated like royalty. As you learn and grow, so will your confidence.

Another great way to gain confidence is to surround yourself with people who are great at what they do. Find the best lenders, attorneys, inspectors, etc., to team up with. Allow your brain trust make you look good. When you associate with leaders, you instantly become one. When you know they are good at what they do, it will help you feel confident that the job will get done and it will get done well! When transactions constantly and consistently get done well, your confidence grows in concert with your bank account. That is also a terrific confidence builder.

One last point for this topic. My friend and mentor Bob Burg says, "care…just don't care that much." He calls this posture. What he is saying is with every "no" you get, care that you got a no. Look at it pragmatically and see if there is something you can do to improve it. However, don't worry about the "no." It won't be your last. My friend Mike Benton says, "Failing brings knowledge and knowledge brings confidence." It's ok when someone doesn't need our service at this particular moment. Keep your funnel filled and the "no's" won't bother you. Volume cures everything.

Confidence will come and your self-esteem will grow as you gain more knowledge, survive each experience, connect with experts in the industry and become aware of yourself. This is a lifelong process. Enjoy the journey.

OMG – Did it Kill Her Career?

Tonya Murfin, of Murney Associates in Ozark, MO, learned that you never burn a bridge, even when you have been burnt yourself, and be sure to help people understand how you work! Tonya was connected to a client who needed to buy a home for him and his wife. She started

24

working with them, showed them some houses, and never heard back.

One day she got a call from him and asked if he and his wife had put the search on hold. To her surprise he told her that they found a For Sale by Owner and bought it! Rightfully so, Tonya's first reaction was hurt and anger. Fortunately for Tonya, she was able to hold her anger back and not become angry with her client. It's a good thing she did too. He went on to send her 4 referrals in the months that followed. He ended up moving and keeping his home as a rental. A few years later he called Tonya again, and asked her to sell his rental home!

The lessons learned are that you want to be sure to keep your gut reactions in check because you never know what good may come out of a relationship. Also, it is education for your clients to understand how you get paid and what the time you spend with them means. Still, may someone go ahead and choose to do something else, of course, but you it isn't because you didn't try to help them understand.

Critical Care Success System Career Saving Technique of:

Goal Setting

Very few agents actually sit down and write out their personal goals. Fewer still specifically outline what they want to achieve over the next month, year, and 5 years. It is nearly impossible to work towards a destination if you don't know where you are going. It is essential to your success that you create the goals you are most excited about achieving. Is your goal based on a cost of living amount, a client amount, some other desire? Whatever it is, you need to be very clear on what you want to attain. If it can be measured, it can be managed. An example of a clear goal would be written like this: "By January 31st 2012 at midnight, I will have $10,000 saved in my bank account." Another would be, "I close 3 transactions per month." Your goal can be whatever you want it to be, you just have to be excited about it. It is always important to write the goal in the present tense so you feel more connected to it. A goal with passion fuels the flames when the storms of recession, poor legislation or a string of cancelled appointments rain on your parade.

Another fantastic tool is to create is a vision board. Many people think this is silly because they have the misconception that it is like a "magic trick." In other words, put something on a board and poof it comes true. It isn't that easy and it isn't magic. Not by a long shot.

The clearer your goal, the easier it is will be to design a path to get there. If you simply want to "make more money" the next time you have a garage sale, your subconscious will tally up your $89 and be satisfied that you created more.

Conversely, when you establish a goal to increase your business to a $1,000,000 per year or $1,000,000 per quarter enterprise by a specific date, your subconscious will work while you sleep to insure you are working towards that specific number.

A vision board does the same thing.

When you create a picture, a very clear version of your future, and store that in your mind, both your conscious and subconscious brain will affix that image in your future. You may not hit it exactly when you want, but since it is a clear goal, your brain won't rest until you have it.

Building a vision board is an easy process and an essential part of goal setting. Let's face it; it can be fun, too!

To create a vision board simply cut out photos and paste them to a large piece of oak tag or put them in a journal. You need to be sure each of these photos mentally and emotionally speaks to you, and you feel energy and excitement when you see them. Then surround the photos with affirmations. Sayings such as "When I believe in myself so do others", "money is attracted to me like a magnet."

Keep the board in a place you can see it every day, even if it just peripherally. If you have non-goal oriented friends, family or co-workers about, keep it out of sight. Judgmental people may be a fact of life, but you don't have to give them any quarter. Stay positive and focused on the goals. Pick photos that are very specific to your dreams. Examples of good photos are of a pile of cash, a car, a church, a physically fit person, or a photo of your family smiling. Be excited while working on the board and you will be excited about attaining your goals. I've also had friends do this by clipping images from Google images and creating a collage for their screensaver.

Books
Think and Grow Rich by Napoleon Hill
Accept Your Abundance by Randy Gage
As A Man Thinketh by James Allen
The Breakthrough Experience by Dr John Demartini
Secrets of the Millionaire Mind by T. Harv Eker

Blogs
www.randygage.com/blog
www.harveymackay.com

www.harveker.com

People/Organizations to follow on Social Media
www.facebook.com/randygage
www.facebook.com/harveymackay

Critical Care Success System Career Saving Technique of:

Learning to Communicate

On the surface this seems like an easy thing to do. You talk a little then you listen a little. "Look Mom; I'm communicating." To effectively communicate involves a little bit more than that. It involves watching as well as listening and thinking before speaking.

It is well known, and pretty intuitive, that communication is not just what we say, but how we say it. If there is discrepancy between body language and what is being said people will generally listen to the body language. The way a person stands or looks at you are clues as to what he or she is really saying. Sometimes finding the right words can be difficult but our posture can help tell the story.

When communicating with others be sure you are choosing your words and your body language correctly. Are your arms crossed? Are you tense? Are you looking someone in the eyes or are you watching over their head? Remember they are getting cues from you as well. What story are you trying to tell?

Listening is a very important part of communication. Actively listening is paramount. Do you constantly talk over people or interrupt them? As you are listening to them do you want to interject your point so badly you don't actually hear what they are saying? Do you want to disagree just to disagree? Take inventory of how you treat others during a conversation. Make notes when you are done on when you caught yourself interrupting or becoming distracted.

One way to become a more active and engaging listener is to clarify everything your client tells you so you fully understand what they need. If a client states they would like a cute home, ask them to describe "cute." If they say they want to be close to a school ask them how close and what school. Close enough to walk? Within 2 miles? What is their definition of close? Clarification will save everyone a lot of time and frustration and can very well keep you from losing a client.

Work on your communication skills to become a better agent. Hear what your client wants in either buying or selling their home. This is definitely an art that takes some practice so don't hesitate in getting started.

OMG – Did it Kill His Career?

Mike Benton, owner of Home Towne Real Estate in Southern Maryland, told me that when he first got started he would tell everyone he knew he got his real estate license. Everyone he told was excited for him and passed on their well wishes, and mind you these were members of his family and close friends.

Then it happened. One of his close friends used another agent to sell his home! Mike had to ask why he did that, and his friend simply answered, "I forgot you were now selling Real Estate."

What Mike learned was that no matter how close the person is to you, you must gently keep yourself and your profession in the forefront of their minds. Don't just assume everyone remembers everything and they don't need to be included in your reminders.

Books
Everyone Communicates, Few Connect by Dr John Maxwell
The Art of Persuasion by Bob Burg
How to Win Friends and Influence People by Dale Carnegie

People to Connect with on Social Media
www.facebook.com/JohnCMaxwell

Critical Care Success System Career Saving Technique of:

Ability to Cultivate a Relationship

I attend many networking events. The most common mistake I see is most people approach networking as a numbers game rather than an opportunity to cultivate a relationship. In other words, the person hands out their card, to as many people as possible, with nothing else, figuring that by doing so someone will call them. Networking correctly will help you cultivate relationships that will turn into new clients and referrals.

Prospect building is a referral opportunity. The majority of agents will tell you they received their last clients from former clients. As an agent you cannot afford to play the numbers game. You won't make it out of your first year. Start focusing on the current clients you have as well as those you meet on an everyday basis. If they are currently an active client make sure you are serving them by taking care of their needs. If they are not currently active with you, find a way you can add value or connect them with a resource.

A referral from a current client, friend or prospect is a great warm lead (one that already has an idea of who you are and what you do). You will want to follow up with prospect as soon as you have the opportunity and start developing a relationship where they will come to know you, begin to like you and eventually trust you. You will have greater success in closing transactions with warm leads than any other type of lead.

Treat your prospects (whether they buy from you or not) as though they are your most valuable client. Not everyone will buy or sell with you, but everybody talks. What will they be saying about you? If a prospect ends up working with another agent, wouldn't you rather have them say, "Gee, Bob wasn't the perfect fit to broker my home, but he sure did give us a great education." Now, that might not sound like a glowing endorsement, but it depends on the impression you made and who he is speaking to. Good news travels fast, but bad news travels faster.

Relationships can be cultivated online and in person. I have made some wonderful friends and found mentors via social media. The beginning point of a relationship isn't all that important, but how you maintain it and add value to it is the most essential piece of the puzzle.

Perhaps the most important thing you will ever learn about selling real estate and creating life-long relationships is contained in the following section (I hope you are REALLY paying attention right now!)

Your product is real estate, but it could be anything. What people are actually buying when they use you to buy or sell a home is YOU. They are buying into you and investing their time in you because they know you, like you and trust you (very wise words from my friend, Bob Burg). Remember to always be who you truly are whenever speaking to clients or prospects. Heed this advice and you will never go wrong.

Speaking of relationships, I always appreciate speaking with other real estate professionals and reader of this book. Don't hesitate to contact me at my community website, www.ChristieEllis.com.

OMG – Did it Kill His Career?

I had the pleasure of speaking to Mark Scuderi, a RE/MAX Franchise Owner & Realtor in New Jersey, and I asked him to recall a time when he learned a major lesson that changed his business. What he told me was quite fantastic.

He can remember one of his first listing appointments he was up against a competing agent. So he spent HOURS preparing a PowerPoint presentation for this listing. As he went through the presentation he began to see boredom come over the face of the husband. The wife seemed to be politely feigning interest. Unfortunately he didn't know anything other than his presentation, so he and the couple suffered through 30 very uncomfortable minutes. Mark then understood the need to learn about his clients and what they want. Mainly he needed to invest the time in the relationship rather than in the PowerPoint presentation.

He says today he only goes to an appointment armed with knowledge of the client, as well as their area, and he looks forward to getting to know the client better to fulfill their needs.

Books
The Go-Giver and *It's Not About You* by Bob Burg and John David Mann
The Seven Levels of Communication by Michael J Maher

Blogs
www.burg.com

People/Organizations to follow on Social Media
www.facebook.com/mmaher

Critical Care Success System

Important Notes

I had some other important pieces of information to share with you but they didn't fit neatly anywhere in the rest of the book. They aren't random, but they are important. In fact, these are vital in helping you survive those feelings of fear and insecurity we all go through at the beginning of your career.

I took a survey and asked people some basic questions about the last agent they worked with and what they wanted most. This kind of information is critical to becoming not only a great resource for you clients, but becoming a top notch agent. Here is the feedback I received from them and what they are looking for in their next agent:

- Be knowledgeable about the area
- Be knowledgeable about the contract
- Be an agent who listened to THEM
- Be an honest agent
- Be accountable.
- Be the agent to proactively call them and keep them in the loop.

Just knowing this information gives you an edge. Knowledge about the area and familiarity with the contract is important. However, equally if not more important is an agent who listens...actively.

First Time Buyers

Be extra deliberate with first-time home buyers. They are nervous, overwhelmed and often easily confused because they are hearing so many foreign terms and have to make huge decisions. Find your patience and answer all their questions, take their phone calls and show them extra attention.

Personalities

When referring to lenders, inspectors, title companies and other affiliates to assist in the process be sure to pair up personalities. Do you have a lender who prefers to do everything by email and isn't warm and fuzzy, but ALWAYS get the job done? Perhaps they are better suited for an investor or a third-time home buyer. First-time home buyers have LOTS of questions. Pair them with folks you know are patient and don't mind holding someone's hand. Remember, first-time home buyers are more likely to move than someone on their 2nd or 3rd home. The lifetime value of a client, in our industry is higher than almost any other industry. Treat them like they will be giving you $1,000,000 because over their lives, between their business and the referrals they may give you, you can easily earn that and more.

Referrals

Don't chose referrals based on a "credit" system. Meaning, don't refer to an affiliate because they just referred someone to you, and now you feel you owe them. BIG MISTAKE. Eventually you will find a client that fits well with him or her, so just be patient and be sure to have the client's interest first and foremost. Do business with people you like. Trust your instincts. Get references. Move slowly with your affiliates. It's always wise to "date before you get married."

Take Notes

Documentation is a key part of real estate success. Be sure you write things down that you or your broker would find important. For example, let's say your client asks you to find a child friendly neighborhood. Obviously, due to laws that prohibit discrimination, you cannot do that. So be sure you email them, copy your broker, and let them know unfortunately you cannot help them with that specifically, but they are welcome to drive around any area and see if it fits their needs. Things that can be potential lawsuits need to always be documented to cover yourself and your broker.

Follow Up

Finally, follow up every new introduction with a hand written note. Follow up every call with an email to be sure everyone is on the same page.

Follow up every closing with a small token of appreciation. Follow up on every phone call and email you receive. Follow up every referred lead with a thank you to the person that referred him/her. Follow up is an *essential* part of your business.

When you treat people well, you will be rewarded. When you exceed their expectations, you will also be remembered. When you serve selflessly, you will generate endless referrals and create a business that can become not only lucrative, but rewarding on every level.

Critical Care Success System

Discharge Summary and Orders

You have made it through the Critical Care Success System and survived!!! I hope this information helps you start breathing life into your career. This material just touches the surface of what is available to you. The brevity of this book was purposefully designed so you would not be overwhelmed. I wrote this book to encourage you to begin with the basics and I wanted the examples to show that we have all done something that warrants a head slap. We have all learned from our mistakes and realized we are better agents because of them.

Take a small step at first. Once you start this journey you will want to go full speed ahead in achieving your goals, because you will soon realize what is possible. Below I have included some wonderful people I have met along my journey. I encourage you to connect with them as well. They are authors, coaches, mentors, friends and just people who inspire me in general. I wish you much success and I am grateful to you for having read this work. Contact me with any thoughts or questions at Christie@ChristieEllis.com

Jean Kuhn – Franchise Owner Extraordinaire and she coaches too www.facebook.com/jkkuhn

Julie Larson – Very Creative Coach and Wonderful Woman www.facebook.com/coachjulie

Linda Ryan – Amazing Coach and Human Being www.facebook.com/ryanlinda

Michelle Colon-Johnson – Author, Speaker and Inspirational woman who has taught me tons www.facebook.com/MichelleColonJohnson

Mike Benton – Home Towne Realty and Partner in the Real Estate Agent Success Circle www.facebook.com/mikewbenton

Todd Pillars – IT Guru and Partner in the Real Estate Agent Success Circle www.facebook.com/tpillars

Please visit my community website www.RealEstateAgentCemetery.com to see what I uncovered while I was investigating the deaths of several real estate agents' careers.

Acknowledgments

There are so many amazing people in my life, I just feel utterly blessed. First, huge thanks to my husband Eddie, and my twin daughters Ashley and Elizabeth for allowing me to take time from them and focus on this endeavor. Then to my mom, Pat Van Roten, and sister Patrice Van Roten, who are a never ending source of support and encouragement. To my in-laws, Helen, Bill, Mike and Carlo, you are always available to help on a moment's notice and whenever I need it.

Not only am I blessed with a wonderful family, but I have so many mentors and friends I am truly honored to have in my corner. People like Bob Burg, Kathy Zader, Dixie Gillaspie, and all of my fellow Certified Go-Giver Coaches, thank you for always having a kind word when I seem to need it most.

To my amazing mastermind group, Linda Ryan, Jean Kuhn and Julie Larson, you all made me see I can write a book if I want to! Thank you! I look forward to our Monday calls to start my week.

Thank you to my business partners Mike Benton and Todd Pillars. Without you two the dream we created for the best real estate agent website would not have come to fruition. I absolutely love working with you guys.

Lastly, thank you Rick Butts and Doug Crowe for your amazing creativity. You guys ROCK!

About the Author

Christie Ellis has been a Realtor® since 2003 and has owned her own brokerage since 2006. In that time she has developed new passions in real estate: becoming a coach and co-creating the website www.RealEstateAgentSuccessCircle.com, focusing on helping real estate agents build the best real estate practice possible by offering an abundant amount of resources and education.

Christie currently lives in Phoenix with her husband Eddie, twin daughters Ashley and Elizabeth, and their mini Australian Shepherd, Dallas.

If you have any questions you can reach Christie at Christie@ChristieEllis.com, or her phone number 480-201-3575. You can also visit her website, read her blog, and find great workshops available www.ChristieEllis.com